Laity Lifelines

Four Services Celebrating Laity

Katherine Bailey Babb

CSS Publishing Company, Inc., Lima, Ohio

LAITY LIFELINES

Copyright © 2001 by
CSS Publishing Company, Inc.
Lima, Ohio

The original purchaser may photocopy material in this publication for use as it was intended (i.e., worship material for worship use; educational material for classroom use; dramatic material for staging or production). No additional permission is required from the publisher for such copying by the original purchaser only. Inquiries should be addressed to: Permissions, CSS Publishing Company, Inc., P.O. Box 4503, Lima, Ohio 45802-4503.

Scripture quotations marked (NRSV) are from the *New Revised Standard Version of the Bible*, copyright 1989 by the Division of Christian Education of the National Council of the Churches of Christ in the USA. Used by permission.

Scripture quotations marked (TLB) are taken from *The Living Bible* © 1971. Used by permission of Tyndale House Publishers, Inc., Wheaton, IL 60189. All rights reserved.

For more information about CSS Publishing Company resources, visit our website at www.csspub.com.

ISBN 0-7880-1879-5   PRINTED IN U.S.A.

*For the laity of
Burlington United Methodist Church,
who are willing to experiment!*

Table Of Contents

Introduction 7

Laity Sunday Worship Services

1. Laity: The "Orchestration" Of The Church 9

2. Vine And Branches 27

3. One Body, One Bread 49

4. The Church Is A Kaleidoscope 67

Introduction

"Help! It's Laity Sunday! What shall we do?" We've heard this call of panic through the years in small and mid-sized churches. That one Sunday a year when lay members "take over" the service can be overwhelming to people who aren't used to the planning and production of an entire church service. The four services in this book were created in response to the need for easy-to-produce services. Each service is complete in itself, with an order of worship, prayers, responses, staging and props, suggested music, children's sermon, and complete script and worship bulletin for the services.

Each service has its own theme, but the common thread is twofold: to celebrate and encourage the laity in your church, and to build a sense of unity and purpose as members of the body of Christ on earth.

This is real help for those looking for exciting and inspirational worship experiences for their churches on Laity Sunday.

Scripted Worship Service

Laity: The "Orchestration" Of The Church

This service uses the theme of the church members all being part of an orchestra, and uses a slide show to celebrate all the lay ministries of the church. The minister reads a script with two lay members while slides are being shown.

This service will need to be planned with *enough time given ahead* for someone to take slides — and get them processed and returned! — during Sunday school, choir practices and performances, youth group meetings, committee meetings, church services, and informal settings (see script for exact settings). The script can be added to or deleted from, depending on ministries and persons that a church chooses to acknowledge.

The service includes parts for several speakers, or may be limited to one lay leader facilitating the service. Hymns and times for special music are suggested, but these may be easily changed. Different versions of scriptures may be used as preferred.

Laity Sunday

Laity: The "Orchestration" Of The Church

Prelude

Welcome

Choral Introit

Call To Worship
Leader: Good morning, people of God!
People: Good morning!
Leader: We are called to be the church, in all of our actions, here at church as well as at home, at school, and on the job.
People: We acknowledge that we have been empowered to be the church through God's amazing gift of the Holy Spirit.
Leader: Close your minds to the cares and concerns of the week, and open your hearts to praise God and celebrate here this morning!
People: We will allow the fresh wind of the Spirit to blow all else from our focus, and we will prepare to celebrate our faith and experience joy!

Opening Hymn "We Are The Church"

Collect *(in unison)*
    God of change and glory, we are amazed time and time again by the miracle of what you have created. We see beauty in the skies and changing of the seasons, in the faces of the children and the smiles of those we love. Free us from our narrow thinking, and open us to your love, that we may continue the mission of your church. Cleanse us and refocus us on your priorities, Lord, extending your grace and joy to all around us. In the name of Jesus, we pray. Amen.

Scripture Lesson　　　　　　　　　　Micah 6:6-8 (NRSV)

"With what shall I come before the LORD, and bow myself before God on high? Shall I come before him with burnt offerings, with calves a year old? Will the LORD be pleased with thousands of rams, with ten thousands of rivers of oil? Shall I give my firstborn for my transgression, the fruit of my body for the sin of my soul?"

He has told you, O mortal, what is good; and what does the LORD require of you but to do justice, and to love kindness, and to walk humbly with your God?

Responsive Reading　　　　　　　　　Psalm 100 (NRSV)

Leader:　Make a joyful noise to the LORD, all the earth.
People:　Worship the LORD with gladness; come into his presence with singing.
Leader:　Know that the LORD is God.
People:　It is he that made us, and we are his; we are his people, and the sheep of his pasture.
Leader:　Enter his gates with thanksgiving, and his courts with praise.
People:　Give thanks to him, bless his name.
Leader:　For the LORD is good;
People:　His steadfast love endures forever, and his faithfulness to all generations.

Gloria Patri

Scripture Lesson　　1 Corinthians 12:4-7, 11-13a, 24b-27 (TLB)

Now God gives us many kinds of special abilities, but it is the same Holy Spirit who is the source of them all. There are different kinds of service to God, but it is the same Lord we are serving. There are many ways in which God works in our lives, but it is the same God who does the work in and through all of us who are his. The Holy Spirit displays God's power through each of us as a means of helping the entire church.

It is the same and only Holy Spirit who gives all these gifts and powers, deciding which each one of us should have. Our bodies have many parts, but the many parts make up only one holy body when they are all put together. So it is with the "body" of Christ. Each of us is a part of the one body of Christ. So God has put the body together in such a way that extra honor and care are given to those parts that might otherwise seem less important. This makes for happiness among the parts, so that the parts have the same care for each other that they do for themselves. If one part suffers, all parts suffer with it, and if one part is honored, all the parts are glad. Now here is what I am trying to say: All of you together are the one body of Christ, and each one of you is a separate and necessary part of it.

Special Music

Children's Sermon
*(**Prop:** a doll or stuffed animal with some type of "cast" on it, as if it had a broken leg. This sermon does not need to be totally memorized, but it should not be read. Children will respond better if the speaker is talking, not reading. The speaker may sit down with the children, or stand at an angle, to face partly toward the congregation)*
    Would all the children come up front with me? Have a seat here! Do you see my friend George? He looks like he had a little problem! He was skating at the park, and all of a sudden, a dog ran in front of him and BAM! Down he went, and he broke his leg and had to have a cast put on it. Have any of you ever had a cast? *(Take one or two responses here, but no more!)* Well, George has been feeling pretty sorry for himself. Maybe you did, too, when you had a cast. Is it hard to do regular things, like walk and get dressed, and play, and sit in the car? It surely is! When any part of the body is hurt, the whole body feels it. But when all the parts are working right, the whole body feels great! Our Bible lesson just told us that the church is the "body of Christ," and that we all have to work together to do the things God wants us to do.

Scripture Lesson John 18:20-26 (NRSV)

[Jesus prayed,] "I ask not only on behalf of these, but also on behalf of those who will believe in me through their word, that they may all be one. As you, Father, are in me and I am in you, may they also be in us, so that the world may believe that you have sent me. The glory that you have given me I have given them, so that they may be one, as we are one, I in them and you in me, that they may become completely one, so that the world may know that you have sent me and have loved them even as you have loved me. Father, I desire that those also, whom you have given me, may be with me where I am, to see my glory, which you have given me because you loved me before the foundation of the world. Righteous Father, the world does not know you, but I know you; and these know that you have sent me. I made your name known to them, and I will make it known, so that the love with which you have loved me may be in them, and I in them."

Sermon Laity: The "Orchestration" Of The Church
(Sermon script follows the outline of the service)

Pastoral Prayer

Heavenly Father, we thank you for the beautiful music made by people of this church. Thank you for the music you create within each of us. Please help us to listen to your direction in all things, and draw us close to you. We pray especially at this time for those in our church who are ill or who are afraid, lonely, depressed, angry, or alone. Please comfort them with your love, and help us to know how to show your love to the people we see in pain around us. Bless the laity of this church, as well as the minister(s). In Jesus' name we pray. Amen.

Hymn Of Invitation "Lord, You Have Come To The Lakeshore"

Passing Of The Peace
Leader: As members of this worshiping body of Christ here in _____ *(church name)*, please greet one another with signs of peace and love. May the peace of Christ be always with you.
People: And also with you.
(People turn and greet one another)

Offering
  As Christians and lay members of the church, we believe that all good gifts come from God. Consider the good gifts that you have been given as you make your tithe or offering to the church today. Will the ushers come forward, please? *(When they are in front, pray)* Father, thank you for your bountiful care and goodness toward us. Thank you for all the money, time, energy, creativity, love, and dedication shared by the people of this church today and all through the year. Amen.

Offertory

Doxology

Hymn Of Closing   "We've A Story To Tell To The Nations"

Benediction
Leader: Go now in peace to spread the music of the gospel to a world in need of songs of hope.
People: We go in joy, led forth in the grace and peace of our Lord.
All: **Amen!**

Choral Benediction

Postlude

Sermon Script

Laity: The "Orchestration" Of The Church

Three readers: 2 Lay Members (LM 1 and LM 2) and a Minister

LM 1: Welcome, everyone, to Laity Sunday. We're here to celebrate the church, and the wonderful ministries within it.

Minister: Well, thank you, _____ *(LM 1)*. "Wonderful ministries"? I didn't know you cared ...

LM 2: Uh, Pastor, excuse me — we aren't exactly talking about you today.

Minister: You're not? But he/she just said ...

LM 1: Sorry, Pastor, he/she's right. Today we want to talk about the ministry of the laity ...

LM 2: That's all the REST of the people here in our church.

LM 1: Right. So, _____ *(LM 2)*, what do you think makes this church so special?

Minister: The minister, right?

LM 1: I was talking to _____ *(LM 2)*!

Minister: Fine, fine. I was only kidding! I just want to feel appreciated!

LM 2: We all do, Pastor. And we're here today to applaud the work of all those people who have been doing jobs in the church for years — even decades, some of them!

LM 1: We heard the scripture about how we are all members of the body of Christ. I've been thinking of another analogy — if our bodies are "instruments" of Christ, then we're kind of like an orchestra, making a joyful noise with our work and our presence here at _____ *(name of church)*.

LM 2: An orchestra, huh? Well, we are definitely a music-loving group!

Slide 1: Men's Group singing

Minister: Look at those guys! We did enjoy hearing them sing!

Slide 2: Adult Choir

LM 1: The choir's music every Sunday adds such a wonderful dimension to the Sunday services. Some days I feel like we don't even need a sermon!

Minister: Excuse me?

Slide 3: Children's Choir

LM 1: Hearing the children makes all of us feel a bit closer to the Creator, Pastor. No reflection on your preaching, of course ...

Slide 4: Junior or Youth Choir

LM 2: Figuring out what music to sing, putting in hours of practice time — it really is a ministry!

Slide 5: More choir shots and/or other directors, etc.

LM 1: The musicians in this church give a lot of themselves, including all those who direct, those who sing, and those who play instruments.

Slide 6: *High School Bell Choir (or other musical group)*

Minister: I happen to know that's true.

Slide 7: *Junior High Bell Choir (or other musical group)*

Minister: Every week, those faithful singers, ringers, and keyboard experts show up, rain or shine, to do their thing.

Slide 8: *Chime Players (or other musical group)*

LM 1: Maybe we *are* a bit like an orchestra in this church; there is definitely a lot of music going on!

Slide 9: *Adult Bell Choir (or other musical group)*

LM 2: The music is fantastic! And we do appreciate all the hours that go into blessing our church with music. But I also had in mind some *different* kinds of singing that this church does.

Slide 10: *Person with snow blower, shoveling sidewalks*

LM 1: Hey, that snow blower isn't very musical!

Minister: Maybe not, but it was music to our ears the day we were up to our ears in snow!

Slide 11: *Lawn Crew*

LM 1: More music, I assume?

Minister: Right! And these folks even whistle while they work, right, crew? I have to say that I appreciated the music that went on in the parsonage last summer, too. *(Note: this could be a picture and discussion of any special project that the church has undertaken in the last year)*

LM 2: That's right! The shovel, rakes, backhoes, paintbrushes, scrubbers, mowers, clippers, scrapers — they made us sing a happy tune! It still makes my heart sing to look around at the finished product of that beautiful parsonage!

Slide 12: *Quilters or Sewing Group*

Minister: Listen! I think I hear the music of quilters ... or are they just "cutting up" as usual?

LM 1: Pastor, that was really a "sew-sew" joke ...

Slide 13: *Communion Stewards*

LM 2: Communion is always a special time of quiet songs of thanksgiving as we gather around the Lord's table.

Minister: But it wouldn't be possible without the untiring efforts of our communion stewards, all year around.

Slide 14: *Other Communion Stewards, or people taking communion*

LM 1: You know something that makes me feel like singing?

Slide 15: *Ushers and Greeters*

LM 1: Yup, it's those smiling folks who greet me at the door and then usher me into the church.

LM 2: It's like being with family, isn't it?

Minister: Well, yes, but you're changing analogies here. You aren't supposed to do that in a good sermon.

Slide 16: *Youth Group*

LM 2: Family, orchestra, what's the difference? Okay, okay, if we're back to the orchestra, then I say that the Junior and Senior Highs are definitely the percussion section —

LM 1: They keep us tapping our feet and shaking our heads. *(Pantomime this)*

LM 2: Partly — actually their energy and the energy of their sponsors is super!

Slide 17: Youth Leaders

Minister: Both of our youth groups together have around _____ *(number of participants)* youth people — that is so exciting to see. With all the talk of problems with youth today, I for one am glad to see our church touching the lives of so many kids in positive ways.

Slide 18: Sunday School or Bible School Teachers and Children

LM 1: Hey, _____ *(LM 2)*, that's you! And *more* kids!

LM 2: Yes, and here are some more of our Sunday School children and teachers.

Slide 19: Sunday School Teacher and Children

Minister: Actually, our Sunday School is one of the lifelines of the church. *(Some of the lines of dialogue may be compressed here if there are less pictures than indicated)*

Slide 20: Another Sunday School shot

LM 1: As important as Sunday service is — yes, Pastor, we *do* appreciate you — it isn't enough to help children or adults really learn about the Bible and what it means to be a Christian.

Slide 21: Adult Sunday School Class

LM 2: So week after week, year after year, faithful Sunday School teachers give us the special gift of their knowledge, time, and love to help us grow in God's word and in fellowship and service.

Slide 22: Adults at Sunday School

Minister: It takes time and dedication to do the job, but it is one of the most important ones we have!

Slide 23: Children in class, or VBS, or during Children's Sermon

LM 1: Yeah, didn't we just have a sermon about Jesus wanting the children to be close to him?

Slide 24: Children

LM 2: Sunday School is one way to let children really know what that means.

Slide 25: Children and Teacher

LM 1: Thanks, Sunday School teachers — your work is a sweet sound in God's ears!

Slide 26: Women's Group(s)

LM 2: Laughter is a pretty sweet sound, too! I love hearing the laughter of a room full of women who enjoy each other's company, and are ready to roll up their sleeves to work as well.

Minister: The women's groups *(and the men's groups, outreach groups, etc.)* are groups who are always ready to lend a helping hand with food, prayer, and friendship.
   The whole church is always grateful for that kind of orchestration — especially when there is *food* involved!

Slide 27: Committee around table, with chair of board

LM 1: Well, Pastor, I hate to tell you, but not everything that happens around this church's tables has to do with food!

LM 2: That's true. Many folks have spent countless hours sitting around tables on committees, talking and praying and working through those practical matters that keep the wheels of our church in motion.

Slide 28: Church Treasurer(s) at a desk

Minister: Some of the music of those wheels goes on at desktops, too. If it were up to the minister to keep the books and take care of the money, we would all be in trouble!

Slide 29: Church Bookkeeper(s)

LM 1: It's amazing to me how many years some of these faithful members have been quietly doing their work behind the scenes, making the church run smoothly and efficiently.

Minister: It's true. All the men and women who work in this church in their many roles hold important positions in this church. We ARE the body of Christ. Some of the most crucial people work entirely behind the scenes, like the prayer group and phone tree, who are always ready to pray for any need.

Slide 30: Persons working with food distribution, travelers' assistance, etc.

LM 2: And the church is important to the community at large, too. We ARE the hands of Christ when we open our hearts, our cupboards, and our pocketbooks to the church and to the needy.

Slide 31: Church Secretary(s) and Custodian(s)

LM 1: Speaking of the needy, Pastor — I think you mentioned yourself in that category occasionally, right?

Minister: True. And when I'm in need, these people are always there to come to my rescue.

LM 2: That sounds like a theme song, doesn't it?

(Slides off)

LM 1: People of _____ *(name of church and city)* — applaud yourselves! You ARE the church! Your lives make a difference to each of us in this church.

LM 2: There was no way to show all the wonderful things going on in this church in such a short slide show, but each of you is making your own music to the Lord in your own way. So many of you serve in so many ways.

Minister: Yes, you, the laity, really do a wonderful ministry in this church.

Your presence in the services, your prayers and pledges, the care and love you show to your friends, your coworkers, your family, and strangers are all ways you are part of this orchestra, this body of Christ.

LM 1: So let's sing again together the last half of the song, "We Are The Church," and look around at each other — we are all members of Christ's church, and therefore members of one another's family. Rejoice — and make music for all the world to hear!

Worship Bulletin

Laity Sunday

Laity: The "Orchestration" Of The Church

Prelude

Welcome

Choral Introit

Call To Worship
Leader: Good morning, people of God!
People: **Good morning!**
Leader: We are called to be the church, in all of our actions, here at church as well as at home, at school, and on the job.
People: **We acknowledge that we have been empowered to be the church through God's amazing gift of the Holy Spirit.**
Leader: Close your minds to the cares and concerns of the week, and open your hearts to praise God and celebrate here this morning!
People: **We will allow the fresh wind of the Spirit to blow all else from our focus, and prepare to celebrate our faith and experience joy!**

Opening Hymn "We Are The Church"

Collect *(in unison)*
God of change and glory, we are amazed time and time again by the miracle of what you have created. We see beauty in the skies and changing of the seasons, in the faces of the children and the smiles of those we love. Free us from our narrow thinking, and open us to your love, that we may continue

the mission of your church. Cleanse us and refocus us on your priorities, Lord, extending your grace and joy to all around us. In the name of Jesus we pray. Amen.

Scripture Lesson Micah 6:6-8 (NRSV)

Responsive Reading Psalm 100 (NRSV)
Leader: Make a joyful noise to the LORD, all the earth.
People: Worship the LORD with gladness; come into his presence with singing.
Leader: Know that the LORD is God.
People: It is he that made us, and we are his; we are his people, and the sheep of his pasture.
Leader: Enter his gates with thanksgiving, and his courts with praise.
People: Give thanks to him, bless his name.
Leader: For the LORD is good;
People: His steadfast love endures forever, and his faithfulness to all generations.

Gloria Patri

Scripture Lesson   1 Corinthians 12:4-7, 11-13a, 24b-27 (TLB)

Special Music

Children's Sermon

Scripture Lesson John 18:20-26 (NRSV)

Sermon Laity: The "Orchestration" Of The Church
Narration and Slides

Pastoral Prayer

Hymn Of Invitation "Lord, You Have Come To The Lakeshore"

Passing Of The Peace
Leader: As members of this worshiping body of Christ here in _____ *(church name)*, please greet one another with signs of peace and love. May the peace of Christ be always with you.
People: And also with you.
(People turn and greet one another)

Offering

Offertory

Doxology

Hymn Of Closing   "We've A Story To Tell To The Nations"

Benediction
Leader: Go now in peace to spread the music of the gospel to a world in need of songs of hope.
People: We go in joy, led forth in the grace and peace of our Lord.
All: Amen!

Choral Benediction

Postlude

Scripted Worship Service

Vine And Branches

This is a complete service for your church to use to celebrate Laity Sunday. The service uses the theme of vine and branches and the visual imagery of a huge puzzle to affirm all the people in the church who serve in lay positions. During the "Sermon In Drama," readers tell about the things that the members do to keep the church alive, and lay persons are asked to go up front with the persons in the drama to put their puzzle pieces on the frame. Sections of the drama may be deleted depending on ministries of the church; you are encouraged to add your own, as well (but don't forget to add puzzle pieces!).

Several hymns are suggested, but others may be substituted. Other versions of the scriptures may certainly be used, if preferred, and choral music may be added or deleted.

Each section of the service may have different leaders. There are parts for up to fifteen people throughout the service, and fourteen parts in the sermon/drama. But many parts may be easily combined for use by smaller groups. When this service was originally presented, the "Sermon In Drama" was performed by the junior and senior high Sunday School classes, and two Sunday School times were used to practice. The adult lay leaders and speakers led the congregation through the service. Parts may be adapted for use with different congregations.

Parts:
    Welcome
    Song Leader
    Leader for Call To Worship
    Leader for Collect
    Readers for 3 Scripture Lessons
    Leader for Responsive Reading from Psalms
    Leader for Children's Sermon

Reader for Offertory Meditation and Prayer
Ushers
Reader for Pastoral Prayer
Leader for Passing Of The Peace
Leader for Laity Affirmation
Leader for Benediction
Up to 14 readers for Sermon In Drama *(see sermon script after outline of service)*

Props:
The "Sermon In Drama" requires a large **frame**, 5' x 4' (a free-standing bulletin board or chalkboard/bulletin board works great!), and either very **light wood** or **heavy tagboard**, painted with a "Vine And Branches" design, and **cut into twelve pieces**, either rectangular or puzzle-like. The pieces and the frame will have Velcro™ glued to them. Each needs to be numbered on the back of the puzzle piece and the front of the frame. *(See sketch.)*

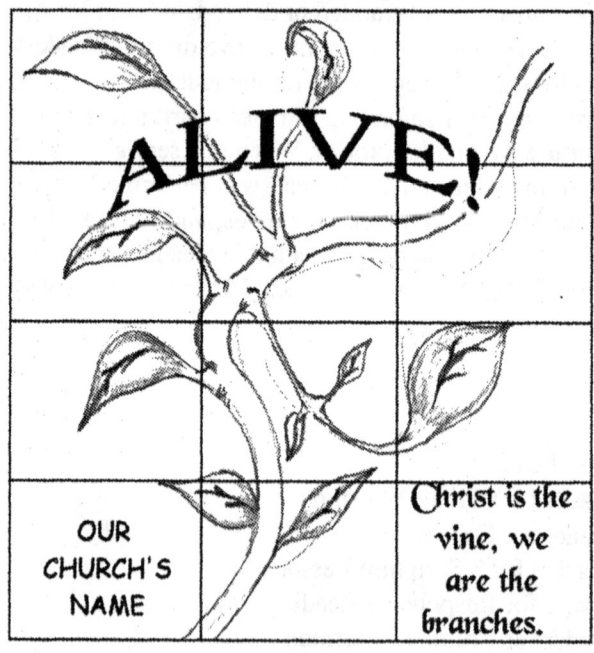

A **wireless microphone** is also necessary, since the speakers in the "Sermon" will be scattered throughout the congregation. One person should be designated as the "sound equipment" person to walk around to hold the microphone for each speaker. This requires some practice and assigned seats for the various speakers!

Lapel pins will be made with the same design as the puzzle, and passed out toward the end of the service, after the "Affirmation Of Laity." They may be placed in several baskets. Suggestion: search computer programs with lots of graphics to find a picture of a vine and branches, then print these out for the lapel pins, about twelve to an 8 1/2 x 11-inch sheet.

A large **tagboard invitation** must be created for the Children's Sermon, with festive decorations and this information:

> **Date & Time:** Right now — and every day of your life!
> **Place:** Right here — or wherever you are!
> **Gifts:** Bring the best of what you have!
> **Reason For Celebration:** You're part of God's family — his church!

Laity Sunday

Vine And Branches

Prelude

Welcome

Choral Introit

Call To Worship
Leader: This is the day that the Lord has made!
Left: Let us rejoice and be glad in it!
Leader: This is the church that the Lord is building!
Right: With Christ as our cornerstone, we will continue the framework.
Leader: With the gifts of the Spirit, with the love of God,
Left: With the fruits of our labors,
Right: With heart and soul and mind and strength,
All: We will *be* the church!

Opening Hymn   "All Creatures Of Our God And King"

Collect *(in unison)*
    We are gathered here together, Lord, to be your church. We are young and old, rich and poor, ordained and laity, happy and sad, committed and tentative. We long to be your people on earth and spread the Good News of your amazing love, but we find ourselves too caught up in our daily routines and the nonstop activities of our lives really to listen to you and to each other. Forgive us for shutting you out of our lives, Father. Kindle in us the fire and energy of your Spirit, to empower us to be the persons you want us to be, and the church that you know we can be. Thank you for the people in our lives who have been willing to *be* the church — your messenger and caregiver — to us. Use us to be the church to the world around us. In Jesus' name. Amen.

Junior Choir

Scripture Lesson 1 Chronicles 16:28-36 (NRSV)
This scripture was sung as part of the ceremony when David first constructed a tent for the ark of the Lord, and appointed singers to sing praises to God. At that time, all of the people of Israel were gathered for celebration and worshiped together, as we do today.

Ascribe to the LORD, O families of the peoples, ascribe to the LORD glory and strength. Ascribe to the LORD the glory due his name; bring an offering, and come before him. Worship the LORD in holy splendor; tremble before him, all the earth. The world is firmly established; it shall never be moved. Let the heavens be glad, and let the earth rejoice, and let them say among the nations, "The LORD is king!" Let the sea roar, and all that fills it; let the field exult, and everything in it. Then shall the trees of the forest sing for joy before the LORD, for he comes to judge the earth. O give thanks to the LORD, for he is good; for his steadfast love endures forever. Say also: "Save us, O God of our salvation, and gather and rescue us from among the nations, that we may give thanks to your holy name, and glory in your praise. Blessed be the LORD, the God of Israel, from everlasting to everlasting." Then all the people said, "Amen!" and praised the LORD.

Responsive Reading Psalm 1 (NRSV)
Leader: Happy are those who do not follow the advice of the wicked, or take the path that sinners tread, or sit in the seat of scoffers;
People: **But their delight is in the law of the LORD, and on his law they meditate day and night.**
Leader: They are like trees planted by streams of water, which yield their fruit in its season, and their leaves do not wither. In all that they do, they prosper.
People: **The wicked are not so, but are like chaff that the wind drives away.**

Leader: Therefore the wicked will not stand in the judgment, nor sinners in the congregation of the righteous;
People: **For the LORD watches over the way of the righteous, but the way of the wicked will perish.**

Gloria Patri

Scripture Lesson Ephesians 1:18-23 (TLB)
I pray that your hearts will be flooded with light so that you can see something of the future he has called you to share. I want you to realize that God has been made rich because we who are Christ's have been given to him!

I pray that you will begin to understand how incredibly great his power is to help those who believe him. It is that same mighty power that raised Christ from the dead and seated him in the place of honor at God's right hand in heaven, far, far above any other king or ruler or dictator or leader. Yes, his honor is far more glorious than that of anyone else either in this world or in the world to come. And God has put all things under his feet and made him the supreme Head of the Church — which is his body, filled with himself, the Author and Giver of everything everywhere.

Choral Anthem

Children's Sermon
(Prop: a big piece of tagboard that looks like a party invitation. The sermon may be some variation of this)

Will all of you children come up front with me? Look at what I have here! What does this look like? Right, an invitation! Have you ever gotten an invitation this big? What do you think the occasion might be? Listen to the details:

Date & Time: Right now — and every day of your life! Huh? What do you think?

Place: Right here — or wherever you are! Wow! Now *that* sounds like a *party*!

Gifts: Bring the best of what you have! Oops! Wait a minute ... the best of what I have? I'm not so sure about this ... What's the best thing *you* have? Love? Caring? Family? Friends? Your dog? Your bike? Computer? Who might want your best, all the time, every day of your life? Why?

Reason for Celebration: In the Old Testament scripture we just heard, all the people of Israel were invited to be part of the celebration when David taught the people to sing and worship and praise God. **We are part of a huge family**, all around the world, of people who love Jesus and want to be **a part of his church.** The invitation is always there, for you to be a part of — God's love is always waiting for you, and HE wants you to love him back by caring more about him than about your "stuff," and by sharing your stuff and your friendship with the people around you, to make the church a loving and caring place to be.

Sooo — shake hands with at least two or three other children and people on your way back to your seat, and tell them that you're glad they had an invitation, too, and that they came to celebrate with you today!

Scripture Lesson John 15:5-16 (TLB)

"Yes, I am the Vine; you are the branches. Whoever lives in me and I in him shall produce a large crop of fruit. For apart from me you can't do a thing. If anyone separates from me, he is thrown away like a useless branch, withers, and is gathered into a pile with all the others and burned. But if you stay in me and obey my commands, you may ask any request you like, and it will be granted! My true disciples produce bountiful harvests. This brings great glory to my Father.

"I have loved you even as the Father has loved me. Live within my love. When you obey me you are living in my love, just as I obey my Father and live in his love. I have told you this so that you will be filled with my joy. Yes, your cup of joy will overflow! I demand that you love each other as much as I love you. And here is how to measure it — the greatest love is shown when a person lays down his life for his friends; and you are my friends if you obey me. I no longer call you slaves, for a master doesn't confide in his slaves; now you are my friends, proved by the fact that I have told you everything the Father told me.

"You didn't choose me! I chose you! I appointed you to go and produce lovely fruit always, so that no matter what you ask for from the Father, using my name, he will give it to you. I demand that you love each other, for you get enough hate from the world!"

Sermon In Drama   The Church Is ALIVE!
                          (Active Laity Involving Virtually Everyone!)
(Sermon script follows the outline of this service)

Pastoral Prayer

Let us pray: Heavenly Father, we thank you today for all the many gifts and graces that you have given to the laity of our church. We thank you for the gift of your Holy Spirit within us that keeps us ready to be your people. Please continue to use us, and help us to be open to you when you call us to service. We ask that you would specially bless and comfort those of your congregation today who are sick or grieving. Be with those who are making difficult decisions, and those who feel frightened, alone, or depressed. Help us to comfort one another with the comfort you give to us. In the name of Christ, we pray. Amen.

Hymn Of Invitation   "We Are The Church"

Passing Of The Peace
Leader: Let us rise and offer one another the peace of Christ.
          May the peace of the Lord be always with you.
People: And also with you.
(People turn and greet one another)

Offering

Offertory Meditation

James 1 tells us that every good and perfect gift comes down from the Father of Light. But sometimes he uses us as the channels of those gifts. Today we celebrate all the ways that God uses the persons in this room and in the church throughout the world, through gifts of time, energy, prayer, and money. Congratulate yourselves on your longtime generous offerings to keep this church an active light to this community! You are ALIVE in your giving! Ushers, come forward, please. *(When they are there, pray)*

Let us pray: Father, we thank you for all the people who work to keep your church a living and vital witness to the community of _____ *(name of community)*. Thank you for the numerous gifts that have been given by the laity of the church. Please bless each one according to your grace. In the name of Jesus, we pray. Amen.

Doxology

Affirmation Of Laity Involvement

Leader: Please remain standing and read with me this affirmation of our involvement in our local church.

People: **We have come together in this church because of our love for God and for each other. We acknowledge that without Jesus Christ, the Author and Finisher of our faith, all our work is hollow and temporary. We affirm that we will do everything in our power to deepen our relationship with God, through prayer, study, fellowship, and service, so that we will be fit workers in his Kingdom. We are glad to be ALIVE in Christ and workers in this body of Christ here in _____** *(name of community)*!

Leader: During this last hymn, there will be baskets of paper lapel tags coming down your pew. Please, each take one and give it to the person next to you *(the people passing the baskets will give lapel tags to the first people in each pew)*, and tell them how glad you are that they are ALIVE with us today. *(Ushers or other designated people will bring the baskets down the aisles and pass them out)*

Hymn Of Closing   "I Sing A Song Of The Saints Of God"

Benediction
Leader: And now may the grace, the peace, and the fellowship of God the Father, the Son, and the Holy Spirit abide with you. And may you be ALIVE to those around you in all the paths you take.
All: **Amen!**

Choral Benediction

Postlude

Sermon In Drama Script

The Church Is ALIVE!
(Active Laity Involves Virtually Everyone!)

(After the scripture is read, two readers walk to the front and read all their lines from the pulpit(s). Others are stationed around the church, next to key people in each of the twelve groups. These twelve people will have the puzzle pieces with them. They will stand up to read their lines, ask people in these groups to stand up, and then walk to the front with a volunteer from that group to put the puzzle piece on the board. Persons performing this drama should discuss ahead of time the persons they will take up with them to put in the puzzle pieces, but have options in case people aren't there!)

Important Note: To keep this "drama" moving along, don't wait for the people to go up and put in their pieces. The next reader should go right ahead as soon as the microphone is next to him/her.

Parts:
　　Reader 1: rather "ditzy" person
　　Reader 2: "wisdom figure" explaining the church to Reader 1
　　Puzzle Piece Holders: twelve, scattered around the congregation
　　Sound equipment person: holds microphone for speakers in
　　　　the congregation
　　Stage Crew: (if needed) move puzzle on and off stage/podium
　　　　area

Reader 1: So, like, how come there are *guys* up here doing stuff? I thought it was *Ladies' Sunday!*

Reader 2: Huh?

Reader 1: You know, it's supposed to be some big deal *Ladies Sunday*! And there are all these guys up here, like _____ and _____. What's going on?

Reader 2: *(Shakes head in disbelief and winces as if in pain)* Uh, *(Reader 1)*, it's not *Ladies* Sunday! It's *Laity* Sunday!

Reader 1: Isn't that what I just said?

Reader 2: No! It's *lay-it-teeeee*!

Reader 1: *Lay-it-teeeee*?

Reader 2: Right!

Reader 1: Okay, okay! So it's *Lay-it-teeeee* Sunday. So what is it, anyway?

Reader 2: Well, it's us — we are laity.

Reader 1: *(Looks shocked)* We *are*? Maybe *you* are! *(Leans closer)* Does your mom know?

Reader 2: *(Leans back)* Of *course* she knows! She's laity, too!

Reader 1: Well, I *know* she is! Isn't that where we started? What are you talking about, anyway?

Reader 2: Listen, here's what I'm talking about! The laity is us — all the people in the church. We celebrate Laity Sunday to give thanks for all the people who make the church alive and active.

Reader 1: Isn't that the minister's job? Where is _____ *(Pastor)*, anyway? *(Spots minister in the pews and waves)* Oh, hi! Aren't you supposed to be up here? Are you a Lady, too? *(Smiles and moves eyebrows up and down)*

Reader 2: Quit it! He/she isn't laity! He/she is *ordained*! That means he/she's been to school to become a minister, and you're right, he/she does get paid to do a lot of things in the church, including standing up here most Sundays. But a minister alone can't keep the church alive! That can only happen if virtually everyone in the church is involved in some way.

Reader 1: Everyone?

Reader 2: Pretty much. Here, let me show you. Help me a little here. *(They drag out the big bulletin board)* All right, now *(Reader 1)*, listen and you will learn something! I hope ...

Puzzle #1: *(Stands up)* I have something to say. One important group in our church is the children. They participate in Sunday School and Vacation Bible School, they work as candlelighters and doorholders, and they make us all smile when they come up front for the children's sermons! They really help the church come alive. Would all the children in those groups stand up? Thanks, all of you, for making our church *be* the church in _____ *(name of community)*! _____ *(Person selected to place puzzle piece)*, would you come up and help me put your puzzle piece into place? *(Takes a child up with him/her to put in the puzzle piece and then they sit down)*

Puzzle #2: *(Stands up)* Sunday School is definitely important! And just as important as all the children are the teachers, the Sunday School superintendent, the Vacation Bible School teachers, and other volunteer helpers. These people work hard to help their students — children and adults — learn about the Bible and about loving God. Could people in those groups stand up? Thanks, to all of you, for all you do to make our church ALIVE! _____ *(Person selected to place puzzle piece)*, please come up with me to put in the part of the puzzle for this group. *(They go up and place puzzle piece on board, then sit down)*

Reader 2: *(To Reader 1)* Look! Can you see that the church is made up of many groups, all working together?

Reader 1: Well, uh, not yet ...

Puzzle #3: *(Stands up)* Since we're talking about children, I'd like to celebrate our youth groups! We have some really cool kids in both the high school and junior high groups, if I do say so myself! I think it's awesome! Would all of you in the junior and senior high youth groups please stand? Thanks to all of you for your vitality and enthusiastic participation in the life of our church. And I get to put up this puzzle piece myself — because *I* am part of the laity of the church! Whooo! *(Goes up and puts the puzzle piece on the board; gives a "high five" to Reader 2 and waves at Reader 1)*

Puzzle #4: *(Stands up)* Let's not forget to celebrate the adults of the youth groups, too. These victims — I mean, leaders — have been working year after year! Would the youth leaders — past and present — all stand up? Thanks, guys! You are all totally awesome! Come help me put in the puzzle piece, _____ *(Person selected to place puzzle piece)*! You're laity *and* a lady, right? *(They go up and put in their piece)*

Puzzle #5: *(Stands up)* It's true that the church is alive if we have active laity. And what makes us feel more alive than a church full of music? We are blessed to have an adult choir with beautiful voices and energetic songs, as well as our junior choir, and of course the cherubs. All of these groups bring the church family closer to God with their gift of song. Would all the people involved in the choirs stand up? And would *(Choir Leaders)* help me put up your piece of this laity puzzle? *(They put up their puzzle piece and sit down)*

Puzzle #6: *(Stands up)* Speaking of music makers, we have some extremely talented organ and piano players *(other instruments may be added here as well)* in our church, who set the tone of the service — the *tone* of the service, get it? *(Looks around and smiles* *and tries to get people in on the pun)* Anyway — the mood of the service with music before, during, and after the worship time. *And work with choirs, soloists, small groups, weddings, and funerals!* Would those people stand up? Thanks so much for sharing your gifts to make the church ALIVE! _____ *(Person selected to place puzzle piece)*, would you help with this piece?

Reader 1: *(To Reader 2)* Wow! This is pretty cool. All kinds of people really are involved in making the church, aren't they? Maybe there is something to this lay-it-teeeee puzzle, after all.

Reader 2: Right you are! And you "ain't seen nothin' yet!"

Puzzle #7: *(Stands up)* While we're still on the subject of music, I'd like to celebrate all those ringers we have around here — bell ringers, that is! They make the place sound really alive! Would members of all the bell choirs stand up? And you, too, _____ *(Person selected to place puzzle piece)*, thanks for taking on this challenge as director! Would you please come up and help with this piece of the laity puzzle? *(They put up their piece and sit down)*

Puzzle #8: *(Stands up)* I'd like to celebrate the activities of all the people who work on keeping this church — the physical part of it — looking good and functioning properly. We have people who work on the building and grounds. People shovel sidewalks, paint, move furniture, make banners and other paraments, organize closets and costumes, clean robes, do dishes, and put up bulletin boards! Would people who participate in any of those activities with this building, or any activities I failed to mention, please stand up?
_____ *(Person selected to place puzzle piece)*, would you help me with this piece? Thanks! *(They put up their puzzle piece and sit down)*

Puzzle #9: *(Stands up)* Along with those in charge of the church buildings, there are many members of the laity who volunteer time to serve on numerous committees in the church, and work at the running of the church. This takes time from already busy schedules, and adds extra duties and stress. But without all the members of all the committees and boards, here in our church, and at the district and conference level, this church would grind to a halt. Would all the people who are serving, or have served in the past, on committees and boards of the church — at any level — please stand up? Wow! That is most of you here! Thanks for all your service to our church! Active laity *does* involve virtually everyone! *(Places puzzle piece then sits down)*

Puzzle #10: *(Stands up)* Let's not forget all the laity who meet in this church in weekly or monthly groups to carry on the business of the church. I'm thinking of the women's groups, the prayer groups, and study and support groups. These people are always here to share the burdens of the people of the church and community, with prayer and visits, cards and phone calls, as well as practical gifts of food and other necessities for those who need them. I'd also like to celebrate the communion stewards who prepare the elements of the Lord's Supper for us. *And* all the lay leaders, speakers, readers, greeters, and ushers! Would all those people in these groups please stand up? Thank you, active laity! _____ *(Person selected to place puzzle piece)*, please come help me with your piece of the puzzle. *(They put up their puzzle piece and sit down)*

Reader 1: This puzzle is beginning to look like it all fits together! This is amazing!

Puzzle #11: *(Stands up)* You're right, _____ *(Reader 1)*, it *is* amazing! And part of what makes me amazed is the amount of work that is done with money in this church! Faithful workers collect the money every week, count it, and put it in the bank. Others work on investments and budgets, and others write checks to the right places. And the rest of us — well, we either give it to the church, or help spend it, or — do a little of both! Would the people who work with the finances of the church please stand up? Thanks, you faithful stewards! _____ *(Person selected to place puzzle* *piece),* would you help me with this piece of the puzzle, please? *(They put up their puzzle piece and sit down)*

Reader 2: Well, that's about it! Now, who did we leave out?

Reader 1: Hmmm ... I'm sure there's some part of the laity we haven't mentioned ...

Puzzle #12: *(Stands up)* There sure is something you have left out! Every person who loves Christ and is committed to following him and being part of the church takes Christ with them wherever they are. Members of this church participate in dozens of local, district, state, and national groups. They serve as members, workers, and leaders of clubs and boards. They volunteer time all year around to let their light shine on the job, at home, or wherever they are. All of you who are involved in civic, political, agricultural, religious, fraternal, professional, volunteer, or other organizations, please stand. Thanks for sharing your time and talent with our community and others around the state and nation. _____ *(Person selected to place the puzzle piece),* please come and help me put up this final piece of the puzzle! *(They put up their puzzle piece and sit down)*

Reader 1: So it's all together — the vine and the branches! And we're ALIVE as a church. Right?

Reader 2: Right! And you can use the letters in the word "ALIVE" to help you remember — repeat after me — "Active Laity Involves Virtually Everyone!"

Reader 1: "Active Laity Involves Virtually Everyone!"

Reader 2: Everyone say it with me: "Active Laity Involves Virtually Everyone!" And that means *you! (Spreads arms to entire congregation)* Thanks for all you do!

(Readers sit down and the pastoral prayer follows)

Worship Bulletin

Laity Sunday

Vine And Branches

Prelude

Welcome

Choral Introit

Call To Worship
Leader: This is the day that the Lord has made!
Left: Let us rejoice and be glad in it!
Leader: This is the church that the Lord is building!
Right: With Christ as our cornerstone, we will continue the framework.
Leader: With the gifts of the Spirit, with the love of God,
Left: With the fruits of our labors,
Right: With heart and soul and mind and strength,
All: We will *be* the church.

Opening Hymn "All Creatures Of Our God And King"

Collect *(in unison)*
  We are gathered here together, Lord, to be your church. We are young and old, rich and poor, ordained and laity, happy and sad, committed and tentative. We long to be your people on earth and spread the Good News of your amazing love, but we find ourselves too caught in our daily routines and the non-stop activities of our lives really to listen to you and to each other. Forgive us for shutting you out of our lives, Father. Kindle in us the fire and energy of your Spirit, to empower us to be the persons you want us to be, and the church that you know we can be. Thank you for the people in our lives who have been

willing to *be* the church — your messenger and caregiver — to us. Use us to be the church to the world around us. In Jesus' name. Amen!

Junior Choir

Scripture Lesson   1 Chronicles 16:28-36 (NRSV)

Responsive Reading   Psalm 1 (NRSV)
Leader: Happy are those who do not follow the advice of the wicked, or take the path that sinners tread, or sit in the seat of scoffers;
People: **But their delight is in the law of the LORD, and on his law they meditate day and night.**
Leader: They are like trees planted by streams of water, which yield their fruit in its season, and their leaves do not wither. In all that they do, they prosper.
People: **The wicked are not so, but are like chaff that the wind drives away.**
Leader: Therefore the wicked will not stand in the judgment, nor sinners in the congregation of the righteous;
People: **For the LORD watches over the way of the righteous, but the way of the wicked will perish.**

Gloria Patri

Scripture Lesson   Ephesians 1:18-23 (TLB)

Choral Anthem

Children's Sermon

Scripture Lesson   John 15:5-6 (TLB)

Sermon In Drama   The Church Is ALIVE!
(Active Laity Involving Virtually Everyone!)

Pastoral Prayer

Hymn Of Invitation   "We Are The Church"

Passing Of The Peace
Leader: Let us rise and offer one another the peace of Christ. May the peace of the Lord be always with you.
People: **And also with you.**
(People turn and greet one another)

Offering

Offertory

Doxology

Affirmation Of Laity Involvement
Leader: Please remain standing and read with me this affirmation of our involvement in our local church.
All: **We have come together in this church because of our love for God and for each other. We acknowledge that without Jesus Christ, the Author and Finisher of our faith, all our work is hollow and temporary. We affirm that we will do everything in our power to deepen our relationship with God, through prayer, study, fellowship, and service, so that we will be fit workers in his Kingdom. We are glad to be ALIVE in Christ and workers in this body of Christ here in _____** *(name of community).*
Leader: During this last hymn, there will be baskets of paper lapel tags coming down your pew. Please, each take one and give it to the person next to you *(the people passing the baskets will give lapel tags to the first people in each pew)*, and tell them how glad you are that they are ALIVE with us today. *(Ushers or other designated people will bring the baskets down the aisles and pass them out)*

Hymn Of Closing   "I Sing A Song Of The Saints Of God"

Benediction
Leader: And now may the grace, the peace, and the fellowship of God the Father, the Son, and the Holy Spirit abide with you. And may you be ALIVE to those around you in all the paths you take.
All: Amen!

Choral Benediction

Postlude

Scripted Worship Service

One Body, One Bread

This is a service of worship appropriate for any size church. It involves all the senses — not just hearing and seeing, but smelling, tasting, and touching! The participants in the service and the people "out there" in the congregation will all experience being the body and the bread as they smell the bread baking, watch people mixing it, and taste it during communion and after the service. In education, good teachers try to use all the senses to meet the needs of all learners — why shouldn't the church, on occasion, try it, too?

The parts are written to allow a maximum amount of participation of laity in the service. They may be changed, doubled up, or split up to fit the needs of the churches who use this service.

It is suggested that the lay members be given their scripts several weeks in advance of the date, and that one or two rehearsals/run-throughs be performed. This will allow the service to flow comfortably for everyone and have the best impact on the participants and the congregation. Since it involves quite a few people, everyone should have a good idea where they will sit, where they will come in, where they will stand, what microphones to use, and so on.

As you prepare a laity service, be aware that the mission is not to be great actors, actresses, or preachers, but to bring the excitement of the Word of God alive in your church. Ask God to open your hearts to the Holy Spirit, and then practice, perform, and enjoy what he is doing in his church, the body of Christ where you are meeting! May he add his blessing to every presentation of this service.

Roles of participants:

Lay Leader: Narrates the service, welcomes everyone, ties things together.

Reader: Reads the opening prayer with the people. Could be the lay leader.

13 Speakers: Read various size parts, containing scripture readings, comments, the children's sermon (speaker 3), and bring forward the elements for mixing the bread (the Gifts). Speakers 8-12 will carry mallets with labels on them to dramatize their parts.

The Mixer: As all the Gifts are brought forward, the Mixer stands and puts together bread dough, until communion begins. He or she should wear a baker's hat and a large apron.

Musicians: Parts for special music, hymns, and choirs are built into the service; these may be changed to fit the church. If the suggested hymns are not in your hymnal, choose those that fit the theme. Some hymnals have theme listings in the back pages.

The Pastor: Although this is a lay service, in many churches the pastor is the only one who may do the communion portion. This also may be changed to fit the church, and laity may also do communion if appropriate.

3-7 Children or Youth (or other brave souls)**:** Pantomime the parts in the sower and the seed story — sower, good seeds, rocky seeds, thorny seeds, birds, and thorns.

Ushers (or others)**:** Take up the offering, pass out and pick up the sticky notes, hold up the cloud, and pass out the sliced bread at the end of the service.

Props:

One or two **bread machines** that have been started long enough before the service so that the bread is baking in the sanctuary during the service.

Enough already-baked and sliced **bread** to serve everyone as they go out the door after they've been smelling baking bread for an hour!

A **table** set in the front of the sanctuary.

The **wheat**, in a sheaf. A handful of **grain**. A large sheet of white **paper** (like butcher paper) drawn or cut to look like a cloud. Lots of small **sticky notes** and **pencils** (if they're not already in the pews). **Honey**, **salt**, and **oil** in their own containers. A **tablecloth** for the table. A large **bowl** and wooden **spoon**. **Flour, yeast,** and **warm water.**

Five mallets, with individual labels: Toil, Disease, Self-Image, Money, Fears.
Communion elements.

Suggested Seating:
Have the "Seeds and Sower" pantomimers sit in the front pews with easy access to the front. Speakers with Gifts will come from the back or sides. Speakers with Mallets can also be seated in front pews.

Laity Sunday

One Body, One Bread

Prelude

Welcome
Leader: Good morning and welcome to our Laity Service, "One Body, One Bread." We are all excited about this service, and we will explain more to you as we go along.
    Are there any celebrations? Prayer concerns? Visitors who would like to be introduced?
    Special thanks to all those participating today in the service or in baking bread, singing, or helping in any way. Let's stand and begin our service with our Choral Introit.

Choral Introit

Call To Worship
Leader: Why are we here?
People: **We have come to worship, to share, to laugh and cry, and to become one in Christ.**
Leader: Who are we?
People: **We are the church, the body of Christ, the givers and takers of the bread of life.**
Leader: What do we bring?
People: **We bring pain that we carry, griefs that we bear, hopes for the future, and faith that the gifts and graces of our Lord are enough for all that we face.**
Leader: We do remember that all of our gifts are what God uses to bless his church and make it grow. Think about all the gifts represented around you in this church today as we sing our opening hymn, "Many Gifts, One Spirit."

Opening Hymn　　　　　　　　　　"Many Gifts, One Spirit"

Collect
Reader: Please join me in our collective prayer of the people.
All: Heavenly Father, we come to you today with humble and grateful hearts. You have made us to be your people, and have given us an amazing abundance of love and good gifts. We ask your forgiveness for the times we have shut you out of our lives, using busyness and fatigue as excuses. Remind us of who we are in you. Fill us with your Holy Spirit so that what we want is exactly what you want for us. Be with us today as we think about what it means to be the laity of the church. Thank you for all the ways you call us, bless us, challenge us, and lead us. In Jesus' name. Amen.

Gift Message

Lay Leader: Welcome to our Laity Sunday service. The order of worship is somewhat different today, as we use the symbols suggested by the idea of bread representing the unity and diversity of the church. The songs, scriptures, sights, sounds, and smells are designed to help us understand how we can celebrate who we are as the body of Christ. They should also challenge us to consider how we can be even better representatives of our Lord. We will have a succession of gifts brought to the altar, with different speakers and different ways of presentation.

Gift 1: The Wheat, in a sheaf
(Brought by Speaker 1, who sets it on the table or altar)

Speaker 1: Today we remember that we are here because the seed of faith has been planted in our hearts, and has brought forth many wonderful fruits. As we see this wheat, we remember that because the church is here, physically and spiritually, we know that Christ is alive in our world today. Many sacrifices have been made over the last 2,000 years in order for the Church to be alive now.

Think of it! A small band of fishermen, a group of dedicated women, following a rebel — who was, in fact, the Son of God — turned the world on its ear and planted seeds — and we are the fruits of it! And people here in this church, including many of you, have made sacrifices as well. We must remember as the laity and as the body of Christ to nurture these seeds and stay focused on who we are in Jesus.

I have some people who will help me illustrate the first scripture.

(Pantomimers come up and act this out as it's being read. Speaker 1 should pause as necessary to allow the actions to take place. This may take a bit of practice!)

Speaker 1: Matthew 13:2-9 — Jesus told them many things in parables, saying "Listen! A **sower** went out to sow. *(**Sower** comes to front, with **seeds** following behind and around as the **sower** pantomimes throwing the seeds from a bag)*

"And as he sowed, some **seeds fell** *(some of the **seeds** fall down)* on the path, and the **birds came and ate** them up. *(**Birds** pantomime eating the seeds; they might then turn into the other seeds or just lay there)*

"Other **seeds fell** *(they pantomime this)* on rocky ground, where they did not have much soil, and they **sprang up quickly** *(they jump up and stretch up dramatically)* since they had no depth of soil. But when the sun rose, they were scorched; and since they had no root, they **withered away.** *(These **seeds** pantomime withering and dying)*

"Other **seeds** fell among thorns, and the **thorns grew up and choked them.** *(They pantomime this; be careful of who you choose for **thorns**!)*

"Other **seeds fell on good soil** and brought forth grain, some a hundredfold, some sixty, some thirty. *(These **seeds** jump up and grow big and happy!)*

"Let anyone with ears listen!" *(Pantomimers stay up there until Speaker 1 is done)*

Remember, all of us are seeds planted by the Lord. Be sure that you don't let the birds, the rocks, or the thorns keep you from bearing fruit for God! Look at this beautiful wheat, and think of the labor that has gone into cultivating it. Should any less effort go into the growth of the church?

(This group sits down. Speaker 2, Sticky Note Distributors, and two Cloud Holders come up)

Lay Leader: Our next hymn is "I Sing A Song Of The Saints Of God." Once again, listen to the words of the song as we sing it, and celebrate those around you, and you yourself — *you are* the saints of God!

Hymn   "I Sing A Song Of The Saints Of God"
(Distribute sticky notes during the hymn)

Gift 2: Grain
(Brought in handfuls by Speaker 2; two other people hold up cloud)

Speaker 2: This grain is here to remind us of those who have gone before us in building this church and the larger church, all the body of Christ. This year, and every year, marks the passing of loved ones into heaven. Practically every funeral we have uses these words from John 12: "Very truly, I tell you, unless a grain of wheat falls into the earth and dies, it remains just a single grain; but if it dies, it bears much fruit." Jesus was the first to prove this to be true, and because he died and was resurrected, and sent the Holy Spirit, the church was created. We believe that those who have died in Christ will also be raised to something much better than we can ever imagine. We remember all of them, as Hebrews 12 says, as a "cloud of witnesses" around us. Their lives remind us how to live, and their deaths remind us that we, too, will finally be with our Lord. The way we live our lives does matter. Every choice we make is an example to those around us, and a seed that is sown for good or for bad. At this time, we invite you to a moment of quiet reflection and prayer about the cloud of witnesses in your life, living and dead, who help you to stay close to Christ and who encourage you in your faith.

(Time of silent prayer)

Lay Leader: Now, we invite you to use the sticky note you have and write any names on it of the people you were thinking of just now. You may come down and stick it on the cloud, or raise your hand and someone will come and pick it up for you. I can look around this room and see many people who are in my own cloud of witnesses, and I can think of several others as well.

(Allow a few minutes for this to happen. There may be some music or not. When all notes are received, lay the cloud over the front pew, then Speaker 2, Cloud Holders, and Sticky Note Distributors sit down)

Lay Leader: We're going to think now about the way that we go from being seeds and wheat to being formed into bread. The first ingredients that go into the bowl are warm water and yeast. And here they come!

Gift 3: Yeast
(Mixer brings yeast, bowl, water, and spoon and then lays a cloth over the table and starts mixing. He or she is wearing an apron. Speaker 3 comes up, too. The Mixer just keeps working as the message continues)

Speaker 3: Sometimes Jesus used the idea of yeast as something bad, the yeast of the Pharisees — their attitude of superiority. We should avoid being too religious or too proud of our spirituality. Over and over Jesus scolded the religious leaders of his day for their pride and hypocrisy, and we want to avoid that as well. But in Luke 13:20-21, we hear Jesus using yeast as a symbol for the kingdom of God! Here it is: "To what should I compare the kingdom of God? It is like yeast that a woman took and mixed in with three measures of flour until all of it was leavened."

Children's Sermon
Speaker 3: Would the children come up at this time? *(Children come up)* Look at what we're doing here. *(Children gather around the Mixer)* We're making bread. Smell the yeast — peek in the bowl. Do you know what that yeast is going to do? *(Accept responses)* Right. It's going to make the dough get bigger! Can a church grow? This building we're in used to be a lot smaller, and it just had part after part after part built on to it. *(This part may be made appropriate to your building)* Sometime look around and see if you can tell which parts have been added on.

What about the Church that is made up of all the people of the world who love Jesus? Can bricks and boards make *that* church grow? What can? *(Accept responses)* Right — love, sharing, money, too, and people working together. And when we're all working as one, and doing all the things that we do because we love God, then we're working like the yeast, and making the church grow!

Let's pray: Dear God, thank you for using us to help your kingdom grow. Help us to remember to be kind and loving to everyone around us. In Jesus' name. Amen.

(Speaker 3 and children go to their seats. The Mixer may take a short break during the choir anthem)

Choir Anthem

Gifts 4, 5, and 6: Oil, Honey, and Salt
(Brought by Speakers 5, 6, and 7. Speaker 4 comes to the front; Speakers 5, 6, and 7 read their parts from sides and back, then bring their ingredients forward after they read their parts)

Speaker 4: Thank you, choir, for that beautiful music. We now have the ingredients of honey, salt, and oil being brought. Throughout the scripture, oil is seen as a precious commodity and a symbol of God's presence. Isaiah and the writer of Psalm 45 mention the "oil of kindness." In Psalm 133, oil is compared to harmony: "How wonderful it is, how pleasant, when people live in harmony! For harmony is as precious as the fragrant anointing oil that was poured over Aaron's head and ran down onto his beard and onto the border of his robe." Jeremiah uses oil to show the blessings of the Lord to his people.

Speaker 5: Jeremiah 31:11-14 — They shall be radiant over the goodness of the LORD, over the grain, the wine, and the oil, and over the young of the flock and the herd; their life shall become like a watered garden, and they shall never languish again. *(Brings oil to front)*

Speaker 4: Mmmmm ... honey! God promised his people that they would be brought out of the desert into a land of milk and honey. Today most of us live in homes of plenty, with everything we can desire at our fingertips or in the grocery store. In the world community, that isn't always the case. But through our gifts to the church and to missions *(this may be denomination or church specific)*, people around the world have clean water, food, and shelter — milk and honey! The other image of honey reminds us of our need for God's Word. Listen to Psalm 19.

Speaker 6: The law of the LORD is perfect, reviving the soil; the decrees of the LORD are sure, making wise the simple; the precepts of the LORD are right, rejoicing the heart; the commandment of the LORD is clear, enlightening the eyes; the fear of the LORD is pure, enduring forever; the ordinances of the LORD are true and righteous altogether. More to be desired are they than gold, even much fine gold; sweeter also than honey, and drippings of the honeycomb. *(Brings honey and the Mixer keeps adding ingredients together)*

Speaker 4: And, of course — the salt!

Speaker 7: Matthew 5:18 — "You are the salt of the earth; but if salt has lost its taste, how can its saltiness be restored? It is no longer good for anything, but is thrown out and trampled under foot." *(Brings salt to the Mixer who continues putting things together. Speakers 4, 5, 6, and 7 sit down)*

Lay Leader: As an offering of thanksgiving for all the wonderful gifts in our lives, we will have our offering at this time. Will the ushers please come forward?

Offering

Offertory

Doxology

Lay Leader: Although our baker is diligently mixing, we only have a few ingredients in our bread right now. The main ingredient is still missing. And that is — flour. We started with the grain, but a few things have to happen to the grain before it is ready to use in bread dough! Like it or not, as Christians, we all seem to go through the process of being refined, pounded, and ground down.

(Speakers 8, 9, 10, 11, and 12 come out carrying mallets bearing different labels. They pound them as they say their lines. These speakers should be as dramatic as possible, and they can improvise more lines if they want to as they're "hammering" their point across)

Speaker 8: *(Mallet labeled "Toil")* Get up! Go to work! Get up! Go to work!

Speaker 9: *(Mallet labeled "Disease")* Stomachaches! Headaches. Flu. Injuries. Illnesses. Death!

Speaker 10: *(Mallet labeled "Self-Image")* You're weird. You're strange. You don't belong. You'll never make it. I don't like you!

Speaker 11: *(Mallet labeled "Money")* Pay the bills. Pay for the kids. Pay for the house. Give to this. Give to that. Save for retirement. Pay the hospital. Buy. Buy. Buy! Pay. Pay. Pay!

Speaker 12: *(Mallet labeled "Fears")* Everything's falling apart. Wars. Murders. Earthquakes. Floods. Fires. Be afraid! BE VERY AFRAID!

(Speakers 8, 9, 10, 11, and 12 sit down)

Lay Leader: We have many problems, and voices, and crises coming at us, grinding us down. Sometimes we feel it's all just too much to bear. But it's part of the process of becoming the people of God. Listen to James 1:2-4.

Gift 7: Flour
(Brought by Speaker 13 who enters from the back after reading his/her lines)

Speaker 13: My brothers and sisters, whenever you face trials of any kind, consider it nothing but joy, because you know that the testing of your faith produces endurance; and let endurance have its full effect, so that you may be mature and complete, lacking in nothing. *(Walks down and hands flour to Mixer, then sits down)*

Lay Leader: While the flour, representing all our trials and the endurance and faith that came with it, is mixed into the bread, let's stand and read our responsive reading, Psalm 124.

Responsive Reading   Psalm 124 (NRSV)
Leader: If it had not the LORD who was on our side — let Israel now say —
People: **If it had not been the LORD who was on our side, when our enemies attacked us, then they would have swallowed us up alive, when their anger was kindled against us;**
Leader: Then the flood would have swept us away, the torrent would have gone over us;
People: **Then over us would have gone the raging waters.**
Leader: Blessed be the LORD, who has not given us as prey to their teeth.

People: **We have escaped like a bird from the snare of the fowlers;**
Leader: The snare is broken, and we have escaped.
People: **Our help is in the name of the LORD, who made heaven and earth.**

Lay Leader: The bread is being mixed. And we, all the varied parts of the mix, are also being blended into God's bread to feed the world. We don't like to feel the pain. But we can help each other through the pain, look to the cloud of witnesses, and know that we can dare to hope.

Special Music

Lay Leader: All through the service, you have been able to smell the bread baking. You've thought about the ingredients, and your part of the body. Pastor _____ is going to lead us through the communion service today, and as he/she does so, I want you really to pray for those around you; really hear the words of the service as they apply to you, and be open to the touch of the Holy Spirit as you share in this ancient and holy ritual that unifies the church around the world. As you do this, listen to and/or sing the words to the hymn, "One Bread, One Body."

Communion

Communion Hymn "One Bread, One Body"
(Sung during Communion)

(Baskets with sliced bread should be ready at the doors for people to eat afterward)

Lay Leader: Thank you for sharing this laity service with us. It takes many different people with many different gifts to be the church, and I'd like to thank all those who participated up front, and those who participated in the pews.

Thanks to our pastor, for his/her participation and service throughout the year, and his/her ongoing leadership of us, the laity.

Our closing hymn is "You Are The Seed." The words sum up the service we have just shared. Keep these images in mind as you go throughout the week, remembering who you are in Christ!

Closing Hymn "You Are The Seed"

Lay Leader: We have freshly sliced bread ready for you at the exits. Enjoy! Join me in our closing response.

Benediction
Leader: Go your way, now, full of the oil of gladness, the honey of the Word, the savor of salt, and the endurance born of trials. Be light and life, bread and encouragement.
People: **We go, empowered by the Spirit and ready to be all we can by God's grace.**
All: Amen.

Choral Benediction

Postlude

Worship Bulletin

Laity Sunday

One Body, One Bread

Prelude

Welcome

Choral Introit

Call To Worship
Leader: Why are we here?
People: We have come to worship, to share, to laugh and cry, and to become one in Christ.
Leader: Who are we?
People: We are the church, the body of Christ, the givers and takers of the bread of life.
Leader: What do we bring?
People: We bring pain that we carry, griefs that we bear, hopes for the future, and faith that the gifts and graces of our Lord are enough for all that we face.
Leader: We do remember that all of our gifts are what God uses to bless his church and make it grow. Think about all the gifts represented around you in this church today as we sing our opening hymn, "Many Gifts, One Spirit."

Opening Hymn "Many Gifts, One Spirit"

Collect *(in unison)*
Heavenly Father, we come to you today with humble and grateful hearts. You have made us to be your people, and have given us an amazing abundance of love and good gifts. We ask your forgiveness for the times we have shut you out of our lives, using busyness and fatigue as excuses. Remind us of who we

are in you. Fill us with your Holy Spirit so that what we want is exactly what you want for us. Be with us today as we think about what it means to be the laity of the church. Thank you for all the ways you call us, bless us, challenge us, and lead us. In Jesus' name. Amen.

Gift Message

Gift 1   The Wheat
Speaker 1, Pantomimers   Matthew 13:2-9

Hymn   "I Sing A Song Of The Saints Of God"

Gift 2   The Grain
Speaker 2, Cloud Holders, Sticky Note Distributors

Gift 3/**Children's Sermon**   The Yeast
Speaker 3, Children, Mixer   Luke 13:20-21

Choir Anthem

Gift 4   The Oil
Speakers 4 and 5   Psalm 45:7; Psalm 133:2; Jeremiah 31:11-14

Gift 5   The Honey
Speakers 4 and 6   Psalm 19:7-10

Gift 6   The Salt
Speakers 4 and 7   Matthew 5:18

Offering

Offertory

Doxology

Pounding The Grain
Speakers 8, 9, 10, 11, and 12   James 1:2-4

Gift 7   The Flour
Speaker 13

Responsive Reading   Psalm 124 (NRSV)
Leader: If it had not the LORD who was on our side — let Israel now say —
People: **If it had not been the LORD who was on our side, when our enemies attacked us, then they would have swallowed us up alive, when their anger was kindled against us;**
Leader: Then the flood would have swept us away, the torrent would have gone over us;
People: **Then over us would have gone the raging waters.**
Leader: Blessed be the LORD, who has not given us as prey to their teeth.
People: **We have escaped like a bird from the snare of the fowlers;**
Leader: The snare is broken, and we have escaped.
People: **Our help is in the name of the LORD, who made heaven and earth.**

Special Music

Communion

Communion Hymn   "One Bread, One Body"

Closing Hymn   "You Are The Seed"

Benediction
Leader: Go your way now, full of the oil of gladness, the honey of the Word, the savor of salt, and the endurance born of trials. Be light and life, bread and encouragement.

People: We go, empowered by the Spirit and ready to be all we can by God's grace.
All: Amen!

Choral Benediction

Postlude

Scripted Worship Service

The Church Is A Kaleidoscope

This is a service which any church can use to celebrate the variety and beauty of the laity of the church. During the service, there are speaking parts for a lay leader, a person to deliver the children's sermon, a reader of scripture, a prayer leader, and a special music and song leader. There are also many non-speaking parts, for persons to pass out colored papers, hold up streamers, meet and greet, usher, and so on.

The structure of the service may be changed and rearranged to fit the comfort, needs, and ideas of each individual church. Throughout the script, changes may be made to personalize each part. Users should feel free to change this service enough to make it a "custom fit" for each congregation. The mood should be celebratory and inclusive of all the groups who are part of the body of Christ in your church. If the categories don't seem to fit your church structure, or if some of the groups you have aren't mentioned, add and delete to make this work. May the Lord add his blessing to your celebration of his kaleidoscope church!

Materials
- As many participants as possible, for reading, speaking, special music, cutting and passing out colored papers, surrounding the church with streamers
- Colored streamers, in the colors indicated
- Pieces of construction paper, cut or torn into "stone" shapes which match streamer colors
- Colored pebbles or stones for children's sermon
- Kaleidoscope song music for musicians, words only printed for bulletin insert
- Bulletins
- Sermon script
- Joyful, enthusiastic, and expectant attitudes
- Some type of kaleidoscope to hold up during the sermon

Color Suggestions

These are suggestions for the colors you might use. You may have more or less categories, or choose to group them differently or give them different colors. If so, be sure to change the words in the sermon to align with your choices of groups and colors.

Green: Youth groups and workers, Sunday School teachers and attendees

Pink: Members of annual, regional, and national conference committees; trustees; members of committees and boards of church; bookkeepers and finance people; members of boards and committees and political offices in town and community

Red: Ushers and greeters; prayer chain members; care and concern committee; morning prayer group; these who write cards and letters; visitors to shut-ins, hospitals, and nursing homes

Purple: Lay preachers and leaders, teachers, liturgy readers, communion deacons, candlelighters, missionaries

Yellow: Givers of donations to church, missions, and special offerings

Orange: Choirs and musicians

Blue: Members of women's and men's groups, helpers with mailings, service organization members

Advance Preparations

Sometime before the service, have the choir, a soloist, or song leader practice "The Kaleidoscope Song" so that it will go smoothly during the service. The tempo should be peppy. If your church does such things, you could run through the song with the congregation ten minutes before the service.

Also, sometime before the service, the people who will be working with the crepe paper streamers need to practice at least one time, if not more. Some likely candidates are the youth groups or Sunday School students. You'll want to experiment with how many colors you need (according to your categories), and how many people can do that.

We had seven young people, each holding one color in one hand and another color in the other, so that the streamers went in a circle all around the pews of the sanctuary. This took some positioning and practice to get the logistics. They have to decide, for instance, how to *get* to those positions, and then how to hold and wave the colors at the right times in sync with the person holding the other end of that color. It took us about fifteen minutes to get it all figured out, and we did it in the Sunday School time before church.

Before Worship

About five to ten minutes before the service starts, have the lay leader or other volunteer go to the front to read the categories and colors, and have people raise their hands for each category to which they belong. Have youth or Sunday School children pass out the papers to people as they raise their hands. An example of what the lay leader could say follows.

Lay Leader: Today we will celebrate all the ways that we, the laity, participate in our church. We would like each of you to be recognized for your contributions. As I read the categories of gifts and graces, please raise your hand and we will bring you your colored paper "stones" for your part of the kaleidoscope. Save them to raise proudly later in the service, during the sermon.

Please take a GREEN stone if you are a Youth Group member or worker, a Sunday School teacher, or attendee. *(Give time for workers to distribute these, then go on)*

Take a PINK stone if you are or have been a member of any annual, regional, or national conference committees; a trustee; a member of any committee or boards of this church, a bookkeeper or finance person; a member of boards and committees and political offices in our town or community. *(Give time for workers to distribute these, then go on)*

Take a RED stone if you are or have been an usher or greeter; a member of a prayer chain; a worker in the care and concern group; a participant in the morning prayer group; if you write cards and letters; or visit shut-ins and people in hospitals and nursing homes or visitors to the church. *(Give time for workers to distribute these, then go on)*

Take a PURPLE stone if you are or have been a lay preacher, teacher, reader, or speaker; a communion deacon, candlelighter, or missionary. *(Give time for workers to distribute these, then go on)*

Take a YELLOW stone if you are or have been a giver of donations to church and special offerings or memorial funds. *(Give time for workers to distribute these, then go on)*

Take an ORANGE stone if you are or have been a member of one of the choirs, or have shared your musical gifts on the piano, organ, or as a singer. *(Give time for workers to distribute these, then go on)*

Take a BLUE stone if you are a member of the men's or women's groups within the church; if you help with letters and newsletters; if you have created banners, paraments, or artwork for the church; if you belong to service organizations in the local community. *(Give time for workers to distribute these)*

Laity Sunday

The Church Is A Kaleidoscope

Prelude

Welcome

Choral Introit

Call To Worship
Leader: We have come here to seek God, to find him and worship him.
People: **We have come to bring the fragments of our lives and hold them up to the light of his love.**
Leader: We have come to be amazed at the result.
People: **When his light comes through all those fragments it breaks upon us in all the colors of the rainbow.**
Leader: We have come to place our fragments together for him to patch and heal us in all our pain and grief, joys, and celebrations.
People: **We have come to celebrate our own gifts and the gifts others have shared with us, and the possibilities of who we can become together as Christ's body on this earth.**

Opening Hymn   "All Creatures Of Our God And King"

Collect *(in unison)*
Creator God, we confess that we do not give our lives over to the transforming power of your Spirit to call out the gifts of each one of us and to build up the life of the whole church. Today as we wonder at your creation in the world around us, may we also open ourselves to the new creation you desire to bring about within and among us, through the grace of Jesus Christ, our Lord and Savior. Amen.

Scripture Lesson   1 Peter 2:2-10 (NRSV)
  Like newborn infants, long for the pure, spiritual milk, so that by it you may grow into salvation — if indeed you have tasted that the Lord is good.
  Come to him, a living stone, though rejected by mortals yet chosen and precious in God's sight, and like living stones, let yourselves be built into a spiritual house to be a holy priesthood, to offer spiritual sacrifices acceptable to God through Jesus Christ. For it stands in scripture: "See, I am laying in Zion a stone, a cornerstone chosen and precious; and whoever believes in him will not be put to shame." To you then who believe, he is precious; but for those who do not believe, "The stone that the builders rejected has become the very head of the corner," and "A stone that makes them stumble, and a rock that makes them fall." They stumble because they disobey the word, as they were destined to do.
  But you are a chosen race, a royal priesthood, a holy nation, God's own people, in order that you may proclaim the mighty acts of him who called you out of darkness into his marvelous light.
  Once you were not a people, but now you are God's people; once you had not received mercy, but now you have received mercy.

Special Music

Children's Sermon
(Have a bowl or basket with pebbles or stones. Have each child take one. Instruct them to look at their stone carefully, feel it, smell it perhaps. Ask if they can pick their own pebble out of the collection. If there are just a few children you can let them try it)
  Did you know God knows each of you so well that he could pick you out of a crowd of millions? It's true! God even knows how many hairs we have on our heads! So we need to be thankful for who we are because we are each very special living stones to him! God has made each of us very specially to fit together with the rest of his children. And when we fit just right, we make a beautiful pattern that makes us part of his church! Remember that we don't have to be just like anyone else. We are beautiful and special just the way God made us! So you should be thankful to

God for yourself, and you should try to learn to appreciate all those around you, because God created them, too. We are all part of God's special pattern when we let ourselves do and be what God wants us to. You may have your stone to take home. Let it remind you that you are very special and one-of-a-kind to God!

Responsive Reading Psalm 100
Leader: Make a joyful noise to the Lord, all the lands!
People: Serve the Lord with gladness! Come into God's presence with singing!
Leader: Know that the Lord, who made us, is God.
People: We are the Lord's; we are the people of God, the sheep of God's pasture.
Leader: Enter God's gates with thanksgiving, and God's courts with praise!
People: Give thanks and bless God's name!
Leader: For the Lord is good;
People: God's steadfast love endures forever; God's faithfulness to all generations.

Choral Anthem

Scripture Lesson 1 Corinthians 13 (NRSV)
If I speak in the tongues of mortals and of angels, but do not have love, I am a noisy gong or a clanging cymbal. And if I have prophetic powers, and understand all mysteries and all knowledge, and if I have all faith, so as to remove mountains, but do not have love, I am nothing. If I give away all my possessions, and if I hand over my body so that I may boast, but do not have love, I gain nothing.

Love is patient; love is kind; love is not envious or boastful or arrogant or rude. It does not insist on its own way; it is not irritable or resentful; it does not rejoice in wrongdoing, but rejoices in the truth. It bears all things, believes all things, hopes all things, endures all things.

Love never ends. But as for prophecies, they will come to an end; as for tongues, they will cease; as for knowledge, it will come to an end. For we know only in part, and we prophesy only in part; but when the complete comes, the partial will come to an end.

When I was a child, I spoke like a child, I thought like a child, I reasoned like a child; when I became an adult, I put an end to childish ways. For now we see in a mirror, dimly, but then we will see face to face. Now I know only in part; then I will know fully, even as I have been fully known. And now faith, hope, and love abide, these three; and the greatest of these is love.

Interactive Sermon
Lay Speaker: "Now we see in a mirror, dimly" — how true! Every day we see things happening that we don't really understand. And every day we ourselves do or say things that we wish we hadn't done or said. We look at this scripture in Corinthians and realize how very far we are from really knowing how to love or be loved.

And yet, we want to love, and to be loved, even in imperfect ways. And we want to see the light of God shining through us, and through each other, even if the mirror is cracked!

Here we are, imperfect people, in an imperfect world. But the very fact that we are imperfect is what makes us know that we need God and each other. *(Hold up kaleidoscope)*

I'd like to make the connection today between our imperfections as the body of Christ and a kaleidoscope. Do you remember the first time you looked through one?

It's interesting to think that the pieces of the kaleidoscope are often just broken pieces of glass or rocks. If we held them in our hand, they wouldn't look like much at all. But when they are put into the kaleidoscope, the angles of the mirrors and the light coming through the tube shine through the broken pieces, and make something that is beautiful and fascinating to see. Think about this as we sing the first verse of "The Kaleidoscope Song," printed in your bulletin.

Sing verse 1: We're only stones, all shapes and sizes. Sep'rately, we're not much to see, but put all together and shaken, reflected, held up to God's light, all our beauty breaks free. **Chorus:** A church is a kaleidoscope, a gathering of fragments, of tension and hope. A church is a kaleidoscope, all persons invaluable parts of the whole.

(During this song, the people with the streamers unroll them and encircle the congregation)

Lay Speaker: Before the service today, you should have received one or more pieces of colored paper. Some of you have LOTS of pieces! The colors were labeled with some categories of the ways that the laity of the church — that's YOU! — have served and are serving your Lord and each other. And even with all of the categories, we didn't have enough colors to represent all of the gifts given to this church by YOU, the laity, the body of Christ.

You've probably noticed by now all of the kaleidoscope of colors around you! The streamers around us will help us remember which color was supposed to represent each category of service, because this part of the service is interactive. Yes, interactive. That means all of you have to do something now! It isn't too difficult, but it does have two parts: waving a color at the appropriate time, and saying, "THANKS!" at the other times. We're saying thanks both to the people for their hard work, service, and dedication, and to God, who has put all of us together in this church to serve and grow.

(As Leader reads the following, the people in the "kaleidoscope" with the appropriate colored streamers or banners wave them!)

First, people with GREEN papers, wave them high. Thank you, youth leaders, workers, and group members. Your energy and vitality are exciting and energizing! Sunday School teachers, of young and old alike, your job is a serious and fundamental service to the church. What we learn in Sunday School is the core of our faith in Christ, the understanding of the Bible, and the foundation of who we become as Christians. And Sunday School students, your faithfulness in coming to your classes, listening and learning and growing is important to all of us! Everyone, let's hear a big thanks for all these people: THANK YOU!

Next, wave those PINK papers. These are people who serve by giving their time, energy, and wisdom to local, regional, and national church and conference committees. They work through budgets, red tape, hours on the telephone, and long and sometimes frustrating meetings. Although these meetings can be a chore, the end result is a vital functional church, meeting the needs of many, many people and keeping everything going! (This year, the trustees of our church have done a huge amount of work. We can see visible results of their work all around the church.) Thanks, too, to the past and present church treasurers and financial secretaries, who keep and have kept the finances of the church balanced and accurate! THANK YOU!

Let's see the RED papers. Isn't it great to come into the church and be offered a warm handshake and welcome? And wonderful also to have a visit, or a note or card from someone who knows and cares about you? You ushers and greeters, writers of notes and cards, you visitors of the sick and lonely, you people on the prayer chain, those who faithfully pray for all of us, and those who call on new families with a special care package and information packet, you are truly spreading the love of Christ through all you do. The light of Christ shines through you in each prayer, each handshake, each stroke of the pen. THANK YOU!

Next, hold up the PURPLE papers. Each Sunday, members are called on to participate in our worship services. Sometimes it's time consuming, like preparing communion each Sunday. Sometimes it's scary, like reading the scriptures when there are a whole string of unpronounceable names. Or giving a sermon when the minister is gone or ill — or it's Laity Sunday! Sometimes it's uncomfortable, like wearing a robe to be a candlelighter. We'd like to thank all of you for choosing to participate in all these ways. THANK YOU!

Let's hold up those YELLOW cards. I'd venture to guess that everyone here should have one! The generosity of the donations from the people of this church this year has been almost unbelievable. This past year all of you have given enough to continue to pay the preacher and your apportionments, keep the budget in black, buy music, and donate to neighbors both at home and in areas of crisis. Your generosity has been a real gift to the community, to the local church, and to the larger body of Christ in the world. THANK YOU.

Now for the BLUEs! *(Make this appropriate for men's and women's groups in your church)* You folks are members of all kinds of organizations that serve people, both in and out of the church. The Women's group has a rich history of service, especially to women and children. The quilters keep our church basement lively and interesting. Members of organizations in our community like Rotary, Boy Scouts, booster clubs, PEO, and many others are the very backbone of our community and a witness to Christ in the world. THANK YOU!

The last color we have represented today is ORANGE. If riches are measured by music, then this church is worth a fortune! How wonderful to have an adult choir, a children's choir, and a cherub's choir, and four — count 'em — four bell choirs! Plus wonderfully talented players of piano and organ. And other instruments as well! It has been said, "He who sings, prays twice." I think that the same holds true for all the music made and heard in our church here — both vocal and instrumental. Our spirits are all richer and our hearts closer to our Maker when your music is heard here. THANK YOU!

If you did not hold up a color today, please be assured that you are still an important part of this church. You offer up prayer, singing, laughter, and tears. The body of Christ is made up of ALL of its many and varied parts, and all are important and worth celebrating.

Not all of us feel like celebrating today. We may have experienced pain, grief, fear, anger, abuse, or poverty. We're still part of each other, and should be available to cry together, to help each other, and to hold each other up through the hard times. Pray for those in need, including ourselves, as we sing verse 2 of the Kaleidoscope Song.

Sing verse 2: Cascades of color reflect off the angles of faces of those whom we see every day; flowing and changing, now laughing, now weeping, we cannot fear change, but accept every shade. **Chorus:** A church is a kaleidoscope, a gathering of fragments, of tension and hope. A church is a kaleidoscope, all persons invaluable parts of the whole.

Leader: And now, all of you gathered here, remember and rejoice that you are God's hands on the earth: police, medical, emergency workers, businesspeople, public servants of all kinds: salespeople, businesspeople, transportation workers, engineers, construction workers, janitors, secretaries, teachers, farmers, salespeople, and students.

Shut-ins, you who are depressed, weary and heavy-laden — Jesus did not come to call only the healthy but the sick and the sinners ... He loves each one of us with an amazing and perfect love. He offers rest and healing. Accept his healing and his love. Enjoy being part of the church. As we sing the third verse, let's all look around at this congregation, and thank God for each one gathered here.

Sing verse 3: We're here to celebrate being a fam'ly; Our Father's the giver of grace and life. And as we share here our service and offerings, we're being transformed to the image of Christ. **Chorus:** A church is a kaleidoscope, a gathering of fragments, of tension and hope. A church is a kaleidoscope, all persons invaluable parts of the whole.

(During this last verse, the people with streamers may walk in a circle around the sanctuary, waving the streamers in the air and making the "rainbow" go around the whole room. Then they can roll them back up or set them down during the hymn)

Pastoral Prayer
Heavenly Father, we come in humility before you. You have known us from before time, and have shaped us into living stones for you. Forgive us for questioning how and why our lives take the course that they do, and help us to trust in you, that the church you are building through us will be strong and beautiful. Open our hearts to your love, your comfort, and your instruction. Help us to be willing to help those around us and to be your church in a hurting world. In the name of Jesus our Lord and the cornerstone of our faith. Amen.

Hymn Of Invitation   "I Sing A Song Of The Saints Of God"

Passing Of The Peace
Leader: As members of this worshiping body of Christ here, please greet one another with signs of peace and love. May the peace of Christ be always with you.
People: And also with you.
(People turn and greet one another)

Special Music

Offering

Offertory

Doxology

Hymn Of Invitation   "Amazing Grace"

Benediction
Leader: Go back out into the world, as beacons of life, love, and light.
People: We go, as living stones, ready to be built into God's vision of the future.
All: Amen!

Choral Benediction

Postlude

The Kaleidoscope Song

Katherine V. Bailey Babb

©1994, 1999 Katherine V. Babb

The Kaleidoscope Song
(To sing during the sermon)

Verse 1:
   We're only stones, all shapes and sizes;
   Sep'rately, we're not much to see.
   But put all together and shaken, reflected,
   Held up to God's light, all our beauty breaks free.

CHORUS
   A church is a kaleidoscope, a gathering of fragments, of tension and hope.
   A church is a kaleidoscope, all persons invaluable parts of the whole.

Verse 2:
   Cascades of color reflect off the angles of
   Faces of those whom we see every day;
   Flowing and changing, now laughing, now weeping,
   We cannot fear change, but accept every shade.

Verse 3:
   We're here to celebrate being a fam'ly;
   Our Father's the Giver of grace and life.
   And as we share here our service and offerings,
   We're being transformed to the image of Christ.

Worship Bulletin

Laity Sunday

The Church Is A Kaleidoscope

Prelude

Welcome

Choral Introit

Call To Worship
Leader: We have come here to seek God, to find him and worship him.
People: **We have come to bring the fragments of our lives and hold them up to the light of his love.**
Leader: We have come to be amazed at the result.
People: **When his light comes through all those fragments it breaks upon us in all the colors of the rainbow.**
Leader: We have come to place our fragments together for him to patch and heal us in all our pain and grief, joys, and celebrations.
People: **We have come to celebrate our own gifts and the gifts others have shared with us, and the possibilities of who we can become together as Christ's body on this earth.**

Opening Hymn "All Creatures Of Our God And King"

Collect *(in unison)*
Creator God, we confess that we do not give our lives over to the transforming power of your Spirit to call out the gifts of each one of us and to build up the life of the whole church. Today as we wonder at your creation in the world around us, may we also open ourselves to the new creation you desire to

bring about within and among us, through the grace of Jesus Christ, our Lord and Savior. Amen.

Scripture Lesson 1 Peter 2:2-10 (NRSV)

Special Music

Children's Sermon

Responsive Reading Psalm 100 (NRSV)
Leader: Make a joyful noise to the LORD, all the earth.
People: Worship the LORD with gladness; come into his presence with singing.
Leader: Know that the LORD is God.
People: It is he that made us, and we are his; we are his people, and the sheep of his pasture.
Leader: Enter his gates with thanksgiving, and his courts with praise.
People: Give thanks to him, bless his name.
Leader: For the LORD is good;
People: His steadfast love endures forever, and his faithfulness to all generations.

Choral Anthem

Scripture Lesson 1 Corinthians 13 (NRSV)

Interactive Sermon The Church Is A Kaleidoscope

Pastoral Prayer

Hymn Of Invitation "I Sing A Song Of The Saints Of God"

Passing Of The Peace
Leader: As members of this worshiping body of Christ here, please greet one another with signs of peace and love. May the peace of Christ be always with you.
People: And also with you.
(People turn and greet one another)

Special Music

Offering

Offertory

Doxology

Hymn Of Closing "Amazing Grace"

Benediction
Leader: Go back out into the world, as beacons of life, love, and light.
People: **We go, as living stones, ready to be built into God's vision of the future.**
All: Amen!

Choral Benediction

Postlude

www.ingramcontent.com/pod-product-compliance
Lightning Source LLC
Chambersburg PA
CBHW071737040426
42446CB00012B/2381